The Neighborhood Paradise Garden

By Monique Dorcely

To my students,
- Mrs. Dorcely

This book belongs to:

____

Once upon a time, there was an old lady named Junie who owned a plot of land.

One day, Junie called the children in the neighborhood to talk about the plot of land. Junie asked the children, "What should I do with this land?"

The children said, “Let us build a garden!”
The children and Junie were excited about building the garden.

The children gathered their gardening tools.

The children prepared the land.

The children released worms into the soil.

The children planted grass seeds.

The grass grew tall and green.

The children planted tall trees and short trees.

The children planted red flowers, yellow flowers
and pink flowers.

The children planted beans.

The children built a pond.

The children released frogs into the pond.

The children saw the frogs’ life cycle.

The children released butterflies into the garden.

The children saw the butterflies' life cycle.

The children released bees into the garden.

The children saw the bees' life cycle.

The children released ladybugs into the garden.

The children saw the ladybugs' life cycle.

The children built a fence around the garden.

The children and Junie named the garden,
“The Neighborhood Paradise Garden.”

Draw your own garden in the box below!

Vocabulary	
Bee	
Butterfly	
Fence	
Flower	
Frog	

Garden	
Grass	
Ladybug	
Pond	
Tools	
Tree	

Made in the USA
Middletown, DE
16 June 2024

55859071R00018